Withdrawn

DATE DUE

GAYLORD			PRINTED IN U.S.A.

Action Sports Library

Go-Carts

Bob Italia

Published by Abdo & Daughters, 4940 Viking Drive, Suite 622, Edina, Minnesota 55435.

Library bound edition distributed by Rockbottom Books, Pentagon Tower, P.O. Box 36036, Minneapolis, Minnesota 55435.

Printed in the United States.

Cover Photo credit: Westlight
Interior Photo credits: Firth Photobank, p. 4, 8, 17, 19, 21, 26, 29.
Frozen Images, p. 11, 14, 25.

Edited by Kal Gronvall

Warning: The series *Action Sports Library* is intended as entertainment for children. These sporting activities should never be attempted without proper conditioning, training, instruction, supervision, and equipment.

Library of Congress Cataloging-in-Publication Data

Italia, Bob, 1955-
    Go-carts / Bob Italia
    p. cm. -- (Action sports library)
    ISBN 1-56239-344-8
    1. Karting--Juvenile literature. 2. Karts (Midget cars)--Juvenile literature.
[1. Karting. 2. Karts (Midget cars)] I. Title. II Series: Italia, Bob, 1955- Action sports library.
    GV1029.5.I83 1994
    796.7'6--dc20
                                 94-19868
                                     CIP
                                     AC

Contents

Go-carting is a sport that everyone can enjoy.

Go-Carts—A Sport for Everyone

Go-carting began as a sport for young people.
Young people still are very much a part of carting.
Most go-carts are owned and operated by drivers in
their early teens and younger. Most of the best
drivers, however, are over age 20—and many of
them are girls and young women. Nearly all the
best drivers started go-carting when they were
teenagers or younger.

The thrill of challenging other go-cart owners in
races is one of the reasons why the sport is so
popular. But people also enjoy go-carting for other
reasons. The fun comes from simply driving these
little cars around twisting, turning tracks.

If your goal is racing, you should get in touch with
go-cart organizations mentioned in this book. They
can help you get started in the right direction. If you
are a beginner, buy a good used machine and
practice go-carting fundamentals and handling. The
more you drive, the more you will feel at home
behind the wheel.

Maybe your main interest is operating a cart of
your own design. If you live near a beach, you

might design a cart that can handle the sand. If you live near open country, you might design a cart that can handle off-road terrain.

Whatever choice you finally make, be sure to ask an adult go-carter for advice. Doing so will make your go-carting adventure both safe and fun.

Beginnings

Art Ingles was a professional race-car designer for a California manufacturer. He had engineered many of the racing cars used in the Indy 500. He knew how to make big, fast cars. Then Art got the idea to make a fast, little car. Using his engineering experience, Art built his first "parking lot" vehicle. Although he did not set out to do so, Art Ingles spawned the explosive sport of Go-Carting, also known as Karting.

Ingles' cart was simple to make. He used a lawn mower motor for the engine. He made the frame out of metal tubing. His cart sat four inches off the ground. It had an upright seat. But there was no "front porch" for the driver's legs. When Ingles sat in his cart, his knees stuck nearly as high as his head.

Still, it was a major creation. In 1956, he made his first run in the Rose Bowl parking lot in Pasadena, California. The cart zipped along at 30 miles per hour.

Everyone who saw Ingles' go-cart was amazed. They wanted to know where he got it and how they could get one. Ingles realized he was on to something. He quickly made more carts. As the number of carts grew, informal competitions began. The carts were inexpensive and safe, so people of all ages could use them. Overnight, go-carting became a recognized sport around the world.

By 1957, there were go-cart manufacturers everywhere. Everyone wanted to buy go-carting kits, engines, tires, and other parts. Within five years, there were more than 600 go-cart manufacturers. Some made it. Most didn't. When the cart manufacturing industry stabilized, a dozen or so top manufacturers were left. They were supported by several dozen supply parts manufacturers.

Meanwhile, the number of go-cart shops steadily increased. Nearly all were owned and operated by people who are involved with go-carting. Cart shops are the places where beginners can find out about carts and get reliable advice about engines, the best kinds of chassis, and other cart information.

If you are a beginner, you should go to a cart shop for information. Then visit a track and check your information by talking to some of the experienced drivers. Make several trips to one or more tracks to see who is driving and what kind of equipment they are using. Then ask the drivers why they made their choices. Most drivers are willing to help.

Most go-carts are powered by 2-cycle combustion engines.

Go-Carts

Most go-carts are powered by a 2-cycle internal combustion engine. These are the kinds of engines found on lawnmowers, chain saws, and outboard motors.

Internal combustion means that the explosive burning of the fuel takes place inside the engine. The hot gases from the burned fuel are converted to driving energy by a piston that moves up and down in an enclosed cylinder.

The first successful internal combustion engine was invented in the 1870s by Nikolaus Otto. Though it was primitive and inefficient, the Otto cycle engine gave birth to the internal combustion engines of today.

Getting Started

The biggest expense in go-carting is the go-cart itself. Kits can be purchased at any local go-cart shop. They also can be ordered directly from go-cart manufacturers. Used carts can also be purchased from friends, from newspaper ads, or from cart shops. A go-cart can be transported in a van, in a small pick-up truck, or on a trailer. Sometimes go-cart enthusiasts even transport the go-cart on the roof or in the trunk of a family car.

The main operating expense in go-carting is rebuilding the engine and purchasing new tires. If you're interested in racing, you also need to buy a starter. The starter, which normally comes from an automobile or motorcycle, is not part of the go-cart engine. It is connected to a storage battery, and it is hooked up externally to start the go-cart.

What to Wear

Go-cart enthusiasts must also purchase safety equipment. Jackets, gloves, and an approved helmet with ear and eye protection are recommended. The jacket should be of heavyweight vinyl, nylon, or leather. It protects the driver if the cart were to turn over or if the driver were thrown off the go-cart. Many racers wear full leather suits and boots, thus protecting the entire body. Earplugs are recommended to protect the hearing. All racers must have a fire extinguisher handy.

Jackets, gloves, and helmets are recommended for safety.

Types of Go-Carts

All go-carts have many things in common. First of all, they lack a suspension system. Secondly, their wheels are tiny. Thirdly, they have no gearbox. And lastly, they are built low to the ground. Over the years, many different types of go-carts have evolved.

Sprint Carts

Sprint carts resemble the original go-carts. They have a sit-up driver's position that allows greater control on winding sprint courses. Most sprint carts use a single-cylinder or a two-stroke engine especially made for go-carts. The engines are mounted on the side instead of behind the seat. The fuel tank is located in front under the steering wheel.

Sprint carts use slicks—tires without treads. They are two or three times wider than treaded tires. Sprint racing is the oldest type of cart racing. It combines high speed and short distances, making it one of the most thrilling kinds of races.

Sprint carts can reach speeds of up to 85 m.p.h. on straighaways. Most carts, however, go 40-70 m.p.h.. Sprint carts race on oval-shaped asphalt tracks that are 1/2 miles long or less. Races usually include three separate short races called heats. A heat is usually 10 laps around the track. The winner is the driver who has the highest point total from the three combined heats.

Enduro Carts

Enduro carts get their name from endurance racing. An endurance race often lasts one hour.

In an enduro cart, the driver is in a reclining position. Doing so reduces wind resistance. Even though they have the same type of engines as sprint carts, enduro carts only have one gear. Some have single engines and others have dual engines. Enduro carts can reach speeds of 130 m.p.h.. Most enduro carts travel between 85-125 m.p.h..

Enduro carts have large fuel tanks on both sides of the cart. They can hold enough fuel for the long distances the cart will travel during the race. Enduro carts also have exhaust systems which may be adjusted while the cart is racing.

Enduro races are held on full-sized, paved racing tracks used for sports car and Indy car racing. Officials measure the length of the road race by time. The winner is the cart that covers the greatest distance in one hour. Enduro racing is popular in England and France. It is the most dangerous form of carting. So, race organizations require previous experience in sprint racing before an applicant receives an enduro license.

Dirt carts offer the most thrilling type of go-cart action.

Dirt Carts

Dirt racing is the most exciting of all the sprint classes. It is often held on oval dirt tracks used for stock car racing. The races are run on a 1/5-mile track or less. The competition has three separate heats. Dirt carts can go 70 m.p.h.. Most go 40-65 m.p.h..

Dirt carts have a sit-up driving style. Their tires are wide and have treads for better traction in the dirt. The engines have an air filter to prevent the engine from choking from the dust. Dirt carts also have a front fairing, which is a fiberglass panel that fits over the steering wheel. It serves as a shield to protect the driver from stones that might be thrown up from the track or from other go-carts.

Where to Drive

Go-carts cannot be driven legally on streets or highways. They are too small and too low to be clearly visible in traffic. Vacant parking lots or similar large areas of asphalt or concrete are great places for go-carting. The first thing you need to do before you start go-carting on an area is to get permission from the property owner. Property owners have to consider their liability in case of accidents.

The easiest way to begin is to start a go-carting club. Clubs are often able to work out an arrangement where individuals cannot. Clubs also can obtain the necessary insurance needed in case of an accident. Cart dealers can also help organize clubs.

Hundreds of go-cart tracks have been built throughout the country. A good half-mile track with plenty of twists and turns is best. Some cart shops may have their own tracks. Many of these tracks can be rented. They also offer rental carts that have "governors," a device that holds down a cart's speed.

Compared to the high-performance vehicles driven by racers, these rental carts are much slower. They typically go no faster than 20 miles an hour. That is usually fast enough, however, for a safe and fun ride.

Go-cart tracks can be found all across the country.

Go-Cart Organizations

Go-carting is represented by two major organizations. One is the International Kart Federation (IKF) which is in California. The other is the World Karting Association (WKA) in Ohio.

These groups operate in nearly the same way. The IKF puts on races mainly west of the Mississippi. The WKA puts on events east of the Mississippi. The two organizations established the rules and regulations that govern all the official carting events. They supply information about new products, lists of tracks, information about insurance, and information about local go-cart clubs. Members receive a monthly magazine that covers go-carting events and subjects of general interest to carting enthusiasts. Here are the addresses of the two go-carting organizations:

International Kart Federation
4650 Arrow Hwy.
Montclair, CA 91763
(714) 625-5497

Go-cart organizations supply their members with valuable information.

World Karting Association

P.O. Box 294

Harrisburg, NC 28075

(704) 455-1606

Competition and Classes

A driver must be a member of the International Kart Federation or the World Karting Association to participate in racing events sponsored by these organizations.

The cart frame determines the official class entry in a carting event. Class structures are also determined by age, driver/cart weight, and engine size and type. Class weight is determined by combined weight of both the cart and the driver after the race is over. Different types of engines are used to determine some competition classes. There are other classes which don't place any restriction on the type of engine used. The IKF has over 65 different classes, 18 of which are for road racing alone.

You need to be at least eight years old to enter go-cart races.

Competition racing requires that the driver be at least eight years old. There are various other classes to enter in 2-cycle and 4-cycle sprint and speedway events. At the age of 16, drivers become eligible for adult events. A driver must participate and receive a finish position in three sanctioned events to receive a qualified road racing license.

At each event, entrants are assigned an off-track pit area where driver and crew (usually two helpers) can do necessary work on the cart before the race.

During the race, the driver may pull the cart there for emergency repairs.

Go-carters must demonstrate their driving ability to race officials during a mandatory practice period before they can compete. All rules and procedures for competition also apply to practice sessions.

The pre-race technical inspection takes place at an assigned impound area. Officials have many things to inspect before the race begins. They check the cart design for competition. The go-cart must be clean, and its tires should be new or in good condition. The wheels must be free from defects. Officials also check fuel lines to make sure they are safety wrapped at all connections. They also inspect the brakes to make certain they are operating properly. And they check the throttle to be sure it closes automatically upon release.

Flags

Flags are the only way for go-carters and officials to communicate during the race. It is important that drivers know what each color stands for:

- Green—The race has started.
- White—One lap left in the race.
- Blue—A faster go-cart is overtaking you. Move over.
- Yellow—Caution, hazard on track. No passing. Slow down.
- Yellow and Red (waived together)—Restart. Stop at starting/finish line.
- Red—Stop at once. Track unsafe. Go to impound area.
- Black—Used to signal particular drivers. A waved black flag tells a driver to continue one more lap at a slow speed and then stop by the racing official who is giving the signal. A black flag usually means a cart has a mechanical problem such as a fuel or oil leak, or some other regulation is being violated.

- Rolled Black Flag—Warns driver that his or her driving techniques border on disqualification. If a go-carter continues in the same manner, the cart will be black-flagged and possibly disqualified.
- Black and Orange Ball—Used for mechanical malfunction. Stop immediately.
- Checkered and Black Flags (waved together)— Finish is under protest. It is used to end the competition if suspicion of rough or illegal driving or unsportsmanlike conduct is present.
- Checkered—End of race. Drivers are expected to continue around the track one more time at a reduced speed. After that, they are required to stop in the impounding area for post-race inspection.

After each competition, carts and drivers proceed to the designated impound area. Cart and driver are weighed together. Class weight, cart size, legality of engine, exhaust system and muffler, fuel and tires are all checked. Drivers may not add any weights to themselves or to their carts between the finish of the competition and the weigh-in. Winners are not announced until the inspection is completed. Inspections are thorough and careful. Carting rules are always enforced.

Cart Safety

Go-carting is one of the safest sports because it has strict safety standards. All race carts must be in good condition before they can race. All carts undergo a pre-race technical inspection.

Go-cart races have strict safety standards. Helmets are a must.

All go-cart tracks must have safety barriers.

Go-carts are checked for faulty construction and defective equipment that might endanger the safety of the driver or of other racers. An emergency vehicle or ambulance with a stretcher and a paramedic are required for all racing events.

The helmet and racing suit of a driver must show the name, blood type, and any allergy or other important medical information in the event medical help is needed.

Race tracks must have protective barriers along the raceway. This prevents spectators from being struck by a runaway cart.

Awards

The IKF gives out the Duffy Award, the highest award obtainable in U.S. carting. It is named after Duffy Livingstone, a carting pioneer. To be eligible, a carter must participate in three separate IKF-sanctioned racing events since the previous year's Road Race Grandnationals. The races must not be run all in one weekend. Carters accumulate points to determine their starting position at the Grandnationals. Duffys are awarded in various classes for Sprint or Road Races. The carter who comes in first in each event is the winner of a Duffy Award.

Professional Carting

In 1974, the first professional carting race was held. It was organized by experienced go-carters, Lynn Haddock and Lake Speed. They decided that a pro class would separate the drivers who carted daily from the carters who raced only as a weekend hobby. Those who race for money join an organization called the Professional Kart Association (PKA). This professional class has developed its own set of rules called the Expert Class.

The entire family can enjoy go-carting.

Fun for All

Go-carting is a great sport for the entire family. Nearly everyone can participate, and it doesn't cost a lot of money to get started.

With the proper equipment and supervision, every young person can spend hours on the track, enjoying this thrilling action sport.

Glossary

- Accelerate—to gain speed.

- Bicycle—to go up on two wheels in a turn.

- Chassis—the basic frame on which the body of a vehicle is built.

- Cylinder—a chamber in an internal combustion engine through which a piston moves when driven by the combustion process.

- Dirt machine—a speedy go-cart.

- Duffy—the highest award in go-carting, given to the Grandnational champion, and named after Duffy Livingstone, a go-cart pioneer.

- Enduro cart—a small racing vehicle used on longer road racing tracks built for race cars, featuring a horizontal driving position and one-hour races.

- **Four-stroke engine**—an internal combustion engine that performs intake, compression, power, and exhaust with four strokes of the piston.

- **Front porch**—the part of a cart that extends in front of the front axle.

- **Heat race**—the first competition of the day, usually 10 laps.

- **Horsepower**—the standard unit of power used to measure engine output.

- **Independent suspension**—a suspension system that isolates each wheel.

- **Pit**—the area where mechanics can work on the go-carts.

- **Rocket**—the driver of a very fast machine.

- **Shoe**—the driver of a racing machine.

- **Sidewinder**—a side-mounted engine.

- **Skins**—tires.

- **Slicks**—smooth tires used only on dry tracks.

- **Sprint cart**—a small racing vehicle with slick tires, with the driver in a sit-up position.

- **Stroke**—the distance the piston travels in the cylinder.

- **Tread**—a pattern cut into tires that gives better traction in dirt and allows water to escape on paved tracks.

- **Two-cycle engine**—an engine that produces a power stroke for each crankshaft revolution.

- **Zip**—to quickly pass another competitor.